Published by Brown Watson (Leicester) Ltd.

© 1986 Rand McNally & Company
Printed and bound in the German Democratic Republic

My First Picture Book of
Christmas Carols

Illustrated by Mary McClain

Brown Watson

ENGLAND

O CHRISTMAS TREE!

O Christmas Tree! O Christmas Tree!
Thy leaves are so unchanging:
Not only green when summer's here
But also when 'tis cold and drear.
O Christmas Tree! O Christmas Tree!
Thy leaves are so unchanging.

JINGLE BELLS

Dashing through the snow
In a one horse open sleigh,
O'er the fields we go,
Laughing all the way;
Bells on bob-tail ring,
Making spirits bright,

What fun it is to ride and sing
A sleighing song tonight!
Jingle bells! jingle bells!
Jingle all the way!
Oh, what fun it is to ride
In a one horse open sleigh!

AWAY IN A MANGER

Away in a manger,
No crib for a bed,
The little Lord Jesus
Laid down His sweet head;

The stars in the bright sky
Look down where He lay,
The little Lord Jesus
Asleep on the hay.

O LITTLE TOWN
OF BETHLEHEM

O little town of Bethlehem,
How still we see thee lie;
Above thy deep and dreamless sleep
The silent stars go by.

Yet in thy dark streets shineth
The everlasting Light;
The hopes and fears of all the years
Are met in thee tonight.

HERE WE COME A-CAROLING

Here we come a-caroling
Among the leaves so green;
Here we come a-wandering,
So fair to be seen.

Love and joy come to you
And to you glad Christmas too;
And God bless you and send you
A happy New Year,
And God send you a happy New Year.

WE THREE KINGS
OF ORIENT ARE

We three kings of Orient are;
Bearing gifts we traverse afar,
Field and fountain,
Moor and mountain,
Following yonder star.

THE FIRST NOEL

The first Noel the angel did say,
Was to certain poor shepherds
In fields as they lay,
In fields where they lay,

Oh Star of wonder, Star of night,
Star with royal beauty bright,
Westward leading, still proceeding,
Guide us to Thy perfect light.

Keeping their sheep,
On a cold winter's night
That was so deep.
Noel, Noel, Noel, Noel,
Born is the King of Israel.

DECK THE HALLS

Deck the halls with boughs of holly,
Fa la la la la, la la la la.
'Tis the season to be jolly,
Fa la la la la, la la la la.

Don we now our gay apparel,
Fa la la, la la la, la la la,
Troll the ancient Yuletide carol,
Fa la la la la, la la la la.

GOOD KING WENCESLAS

Good King Wenceslas looked out,
On the feast of Stephen,
When the snow lay round about,
Deep, and crisp, and even:

Brightly shone the moon that night,
Though the frost was cruel,
When a poor man came in sight,
Gath'ring winter fuel.

HARK! THE HERALD ANGELS SING

Hark! the herald angels sing,
"Glory to the newborn King;
Peace on earth, and mercy mild,
God and sinners reconciled!"

Joyful, all ye nations, rise,
Join the triumph of the skies;
With the angelic host proclaim,
"Christ is born in Bethlehem!"
Hark! the herald angels sing,
"Glory to the newborn King!"

JOY TO THE WORLD

Joy to the world! the Lord is come:
Let earth receive her King;
Let every heart prepare Him room,

And heaven and nature sing,
And heaven and nature sing,
And heaven, and heaven
And nature sing.

SILENT NIGHT! HOLY NIGHT!

Silent night! holy night!
All is calm, all is bright;
Round yon Virgin Mother and Child,
Holy Infant so tender and mild:
Sleep in heavenly peace,
Sleep in heavenly peace.